PENGUIN MODERN CLA

This Is Not a Small Vo

Sonia Sanchez (b. 1934) is a poet, playwright, educator, activist, and one of the founders of the Black Arts movement. She is the author of more than a dozen books of poetry, including *Does Your House Have Lions?* which was nominated for the National Book Critics Circle Award; and *Homegirls & Handgrenades*, which won an American Book Award. Her other accolades include the Robert Creeley Award, the Frost Medal, the Wallace Stevens Award, and the prestigious Anisfield-Wolf Lifetime Achievement Award. She lives in Philadelphia.

SONIA SANCHEZ

This Is Not a Small Voice

Selected Poems

PENGUIN BOOKS

PENGUIN CLASSICS

UK | USA | Canada | Ireland | Australia
India | New Zealand | South Africa

Penguin Classics is part of the Penguin Random House group of companies
whose addresses can be found at global.penguinrandomhouse.com.

Penguin Random House UK
One Embassy Gardens, 8 Viaduct Gardens, London SW11 7BW

penguin.co.uk

Penguin
Random House
UK

This selection first published in Penguin Classics 2025
001

Set in 11.25/14pt Dante MT Std
Typeset by Jouve (UK), Milton Keynes
Printed and bound in Great Britain by Clays Ltd, Elcograf S.p.A.

The authorized representative in the EEA is Penguin Random House Ireland,
Morrison Chambers, 32 Nassau Street, Dublin D02 YH68

A CIP catalogue record for this book is available from the British Library

ISBN: 978–0–241–75604–1

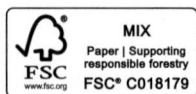

MIX
Paper | Supporting
responsible forestry
FSC
www.fsc.org   FSC® C018179

Contents

Under a Soprano Sky 1

Fragment 1 3

Fragment 2 4

This Is Not a Small Voice 5

Story 7

Sequences 9

City Songs 12

Poem Written After Reading Wright's 'American Hunger' 14

At the Gallery of La Casa de Las Americas,
    Habana. Dec. 1984 15

A Poem for Ella Fitzgerald 18

Poem No. 10 22

Ballad 23

Poem No. 7 25

Fall 26

Philadelphia: Spring, 1985 27

When we come 29

From a Black Feminist Conference Reflections on
    Margaret Walker: Poet 30

to CHucK 32

a ballad for stirling street (to be sung) 34

personal letter no. 3 36

a poem for my father 37

insomnia 38

A Poem for Paul 39

Past 40

Why / Poem No. 1 42

July 43

Father and Daughter (I) 44

poem at thirty 45

Depression 47

(section 1) 49

Does Your House Have Lions? 52

On Seeing a Pacifist Burn 111

malcolm 112

An Anthem 114

in the courtroom 116

MIAS 118

A Love Song for Spelman 124

Father and Daughter (II) 130

haikuography 132

Haiku / After the fifth day 134

Haiku / Haiku 135

10 haiku 136

15 haiku 138

9 haiku 141

6 haiku 144

Haiku and Tanka for Harriet Tubman 146

personal letter no. 2 153

Acknowledgements 154

Under a Soprano Sky

I.

once i lived on pillars in a green house
boarded by lilacs that rocked voices into weeds.
i bled an owl's blood
shredding the grass until i
rocked in a choir of worms.
obscene with hands, i wooed the world
with thumbs
                    while yo-yos hummed.
was it an unborn lacquer i peeled?
the woods, tall as waves, sang in mixed
tongues that loosened the scalp
and my bones wrapped in white dust
returned to echo in my thighs.

i heard a pulse wandering somewhere
on vague embankments.
O are my hands breathing? I cannot smell the nerves.
i saw the sun
ripening green stones for fields.
O have my eyes run down? i cannot taste my birth.

2.

now as i move, mouth quivering with silks
my skin runs soft with eyes.
descending into my legs, i follow obscure birds
purchasing orthopedic wings.
the air is late this summer.
i peel the spine and flood
the earth with adolescence.
O who will pump these breasts? I cannot waltz my tongue.

under a soprano sky, a woman sings,
lovely as chandeliers.

Fragment 1

alone
deranged by loitering
i hear the bricks pacing my window.
my pores know how to come.
what survives in me
i still suspect.

how still this savior.
white suit in singing hand.
spitting mildew air.
who shapes the shade
is.

i am a reluctant ache
authenticating my bones.
i shall spread out my veins
and beat the dust into noise.

Fragment 2

I am reciting the rain
caught in my scream.
these lips cannot swim
only by breasts wild as
black waves.

I met a collector of rain   once
who went to sleep in my sleeve.
is his alibi still under
my arm?

I keep coughing up butterflies
my entrails trail albino tunes
his voice comes in my hair.
is the flesh tender where the knees weep?

This Is Not a Small Voice

This is not a small voice
you hear   this is a large
voice coming out of these cities.
This is the voice of LaTanya.
Kadesha. Shaniqua. This
is the voice of Antoine.
Darryl. Shaquille.
Running over waters
navigating the hallways
of our schools spilling out
on the corners of our cities and
no epitaphs spill out of their river mouths.

This is not a small love
you hear   this is a large
love, a passion for kissing learning
on its face.
This is a love that crowns the feet with hands
that nourishes, conceives, feels the water sails
mends the children,
folds them inside our history where they
toast more than the flesh
where they suck the bones of the alphabet
and spit out closed vowels.

This is a love colored with iron and lace.
This is a love initialed Black Genius.

This is not a small voice
you hear.

Story

in medias res
there came a man into the city
he wore a jackdaw face
and loved the glittering town.
i cannot say why he chose me.
i was the city's device
the city's kept disgrace.
yet he lifted me until i had
a passion to please
all displeasures.

each day he said
o my child,
the world has moved away from love
the earth has moved away from worship
i am destined to end their exile.

        and he returned me to the mainland
        dressed in white. i was in unity.
        soon, o soon, i would be worthy.
because he was good with his hands
he became a technician
where mathematical abstractions
were operable.
thus he caressed two levers that could level
three generations of russians
resting in their squares.

each day he cried
when will they understand the
errors of their ways
when will they touch the godhead
and leave the verses of the rocks?

            and i was dressed in blue
            blue of the savior's sky
            soon, o soon i would be worthy.

there are many cities
there are men in the cities
rooted.
there are few men
there are few cities
afraid.
there are cities
crowded with christs
invisible
there are men
crystal with echoes
indifferent
there are many cities
there are men in the cities
empty
there are few cities
there are few men
worthy.

         soon, o soon, I would be worthy.

ringaroundtheatmosphere
apocketfullofchains
kerboomkerboom
wehavenopains

Sequences

1.

today I am
tired of sabbaths.
I seek a river of sticks
scratching the spine.
O I have laughed the clown's air
now my breath dries in paint.

2.

what is this profusion?
the sun does not burn
a cure, but hoards
while I stretch upward.
I hear, turning
in my shrug
a blaze of horns.
O I had forgotten parades
belabored with dreams.

3.

in my father's time
I fished in ponds
without fishes.
arching my throat,
I gargled amid nerves
and sang of redeemers.

> (o where have you been sweet
>   redeemer, sharp redeemer,
> o where have you been baroque
>   shimmer?
> i have been in coventry
> where ghosts danced in my veins
> i have heard you in all refrains.)

4.

ah the lull of
a yellow voice
that does not whine
with roots.
I have touched breasts
and buildings answered.
I have breathed
moth-shaped men
without seeds.
(O indiscriminate sleeves)

(once upon an afternoon
i became still-life
i carried a balloon
and a long black knife.)

5.

love comes with pink eyes
with movements that run
green then blue again.
my thighs burn in crystal.

City Songs

dope pushers dope pushers
   git outa our parks
   we come to slide on slides
   climb the monkey bars

don't need yo/dope
   to make us git high
   the swings will take us
   way up in the sky.

dope pushers dope pushers
   u ain't no friend
   no matter how you smile
   and always pretend

cuz we know nowadays
   black is a baaddDD groove
   and dope is a trick bag
   for fools fools fools

dope pushers dope pushers
   offa our street
   cuz one of these days
   you gonna meet

some together black men
 who'll show you the score
 and you won't be standing round
 tempting us no mo

dope pushers dope pushers
 change while you can
 it's nation/builden/time
 for black people in every land

so c'mon. c'mon. brothas
 run fas as u can
 and be what u must be
 sun people in a black land.

dope pushers dope pushers
 git back, git back
 cuz to git ahead today
 you gots to be black. black. black.

Poem Written After Reading Wright's 'American Hunger'

for the homegirl who told Wright of her
desire to go to the circus

such a simple desire
wanting to go to the circus
wanting to see the animals
orange with laughter.

such a simple need
amid yo / easy desire
to ride her
while clowns waited offstage
and children tugged at her young legs.

did you tell her man that we're
all acrobats tumbling out of
our separate arenas?
you. peeling her
skin while dreams turned
somersaults in her eyes.

such a simple woman
illiterate with juices
in a city where hunger
is passed around for seconds.

At the Gallery of La Casa de Las Americas, Habana. Dec. 1984

Picture No. 1
Arnold Belkin: Attica

You say Belkin that the bones
keep regenerating themselves
but these zeromen surrounding us
will they always allow us time to
recruit marrow for our bones
packaged in attica mold.
will we always stitch ourselves
together in time Belkin as these
spacemen jailers freeze their
penises in future containers
to be opened in perpetuity.
Stepping back from your picture
Belkin i remember my last visit
to attica the bullet holes loitering
in the walls the sound of bullets
still circling our eyes.

Picture No. 2
Roberto Malta: Chile: Sin Titulo

Comic strip phantoms polluting
the earth with freudian cartoons
dr seuss daddies in crisis,
bleep bleep bleep
calling all saturdaymorning
redwhiteandblueamerican kids
slig spliggety sploo
calling all yall bloods
comeincomein whereeveryouare
hee. hee. haa. And yo mama too.

They're barbecuing ribs this morning
a good sale on 4th of july ribs today
mothers fetuses at half-price
the little black bastards ain't
worth shit nohow.
sitting on top of the world the
stone people sit like pelicans
holier than time.

it's raining clasped hands again.

the acrobatic preachers have
returned wearing their baggy
pants smiles
in the name of general motors
mcdonalds the pope the father
son and holy ghost.
in the name of holidays and genocide:

parades infanticide and imperialism
we bless this wholewideworld
of sports and what's left over
is up for grabs.
to have prayed for a second coming
and found you waiting in the wings
with sylvester trying to catch tweety-bird.
    i thot i saw a putty cat.
    i diiid see a putty cat.
cmon everybody.
    let's dive for cover.

A Poem for Ella Fitzgerald

when she came on the stage, this Ella
there were rumors of hurricanes and
over the rooftops of concert stages
the moon turned red in the sky,
it was Ella, Ella.

queen Ella had come
and words spilled out
leaving a trail of witnesses smiling
amen – amen – a woman – a woman.

she began
this three agèd woman
nightingales in her throat
and squads of horns came out
to greet her.

streams of violins and pianos
splashed their welcome
and our stained glass silences
our braided spaces
unraveled
opened up
said who's that coming?
who's that knocking at the door?
whose voice lingers on
that stage gone mad with

> *perdido. perdido. perdido.*
> *i lost my heart in toledoooooo.*

whose voice is climbing
up this morning chimney
smoking with life
carrying her basket of words
a tisket a tasket
my little yellow
basket – i wrote a
letter to my mom and
on the way i dropped it –
was it red . . . no no no no
was it green . . . no no no no
was it blue . . . no no no no
just a little yellow

voice rescuing razor thin lyrics
from hopscotching dreams.

we first watched her navigating
an apollo stage amid high-stepping
yellow legs
we watched her watching us
shiny and pure woman
sugar and spice woman
her voice a nun's whisper
her voice pouring out
guitar thickened blues,
her voice a faraway horn
questioning the wind,
and she became Ella,
first lady of tongues
Ella cruising our veins

voice walking on water
crossed in prayer,
she became holy
a thousand sermons
concealed in her bones
as she raised them in a
symphonic shudder
carrying our sighs into
her bloodstream.

this voice, chasing the
morning waves,
this Ella-tonian voice soft
like four layers of lace.
>   *when i die Ella*
>   *tell the whole joint*
>   *please, please, don't talk*
>   *about me when i'm gone . . .*

i remember waiting one nite
for her appearance
audience impatient at the lateness
of musicians,
i remember it was april
and the flowers ran yellow
the sun downpoured yellow butterflies
and the day was yellow and silent
all of spring held us
in a single drop of blood.

when she appeared on stage
she became Nut arching over us
feet and hands placed on the stage

music flowing from her breasts
she swallowed the sun
sang confessions from the evening stars
made earth divulge her secrets
gave birth to skies in her song
remade the insistent air
and we became anointed found
inside her bop

        bop bop dowa
        bop bop doowaaa
        bop bop dooooowaaaa

Lady. Lady. Lady.
be good. be good
to me.

        to you.   to us all
cuz we just some lonesome babes
in the woods
hey lady. sweetellalady
Lady. Lady. Lady. be gooooood
ELLA ELLA ELLALADY
    be good
        gooooood
           gooooooood . . .

Poem No. 10

you keep saying you were always there
waiting for me to see you.
                         you said that once
on the wings of a pale green butterfly
you rode across san francisco's hills
and touched my hair as i caressed
a child called militancy
you keep saying you were always there

holding my small hand
                as i walked
unbending indiana streets i could not see around
and you grew a black mountain
of curves and i turned
and became soft again
you keep saying you were always there

repeating my name softly
               as i slept in
slow pittsburgh blues and you made me
sweat nite dreams that danced
and danced until the morning
rained yo / red delirium
You keep saying you were always there
You keep saying you were always there
             Will you stay love
              Now that i am here?

Ballad
(after the spanish)

forgive me if i laugh
you are so sure of love
you are so young
and i too old to learn of love.

the rain exploding
in the air is love
the grass excreting her
green wax is love
and stones remembering
past steps is love,
but you. You are too young
for love
and i too old.

Once. What does it matter
When or who, i knew
of love.
i fixed my body
under his and went
to sleep in love
all trace of me
was wiped away

forgive me if i smile
Young heiress of a naked dream
You are so young
and i too old to learn of love.

Poem No. 7

when he came home
from her
he poured me on
the bed and slid
into me like glass.
and there was
the sound of splinters

Fall

i have been drunk since
summer, sure you would
come to sift the waves
until they flaked like
diamonds over our flanks.
i have not moved
even when wild
horses, with snouts like pigs,
came to violate me,
i squatted in
my baptism.
O hear the sea
galloping like stallions
toward spring.

Philadelphia: Spring, 1985

I.

/a phila. fireman reflects after
seeing a decapitated body in the MOVE ruins/

to see those eyes
orange like butterflies
over the walls.

i must move away
from this little-ease
where the pulse
shrinks into itself
and carve myself in white.

O to press the seasons
and taste the quiet juice
of their veins.

2. */memory/*

  a.
Thus in the varicose town
where eyes splintered the night with glass
the children touched at random
sat in places where legions rode.

And O we watched the young birds
stretch the sky
until it streamed white ashes
and O we saw mountains lean on seas
to drink the blood of whales
then wander dumb with their wet bowels.

    b.
Everywhere young
faces breathing in crusts.
breakfast of dreams.
The city, lit by a single fire,
followed the air into disorder.
And the sabbath stones singed our eyes
with each morning's coin.

    c.
Praise of a cureless death they heard
without confessor;
Praise of cathedrals
pressing their genesis from priests;
Praise of wild gulls who came and drank
their summer's milk,
then led them toward the parish snow.

How still the spiderless city.
The earth is immemorial in death.

When we come

When we come
riden our green horses
against the tenement dust,
when we come, tall as waves,
holden our black/brown/
high yellow/tomorrows,
then you will hear young hooves
thunderen in space
and we will rise with
rainbows from the sea
to silence
our yesterday blues

when we come
riden our green breath
against the morning sky.

From a Black Feminist Conference
Reflections on Margaret Walker: Poet

chicago/october 1977/saturday afternoon/
margaret walker walks her red clay mississippi walk
into a room of feminists. a strong gust of a woman,
raining warm honeysuckle kisses and smiles. and i
fold myself into her and hear a primordial black
song sailing down the guinea coast.

her face. ordained with lines. confesses poems.
halleluyas. choruses. she turns leans her crane like
neck on the edge of the world, emphasizing us.
in this hotel/village/room. heavy with women. our
names become known to us.

there is an echo about her. of black people rhyming
of a woman celebrating herself and a people. words
ripen on her mouth like pomegranates. this pecan/
color/woman. short limbed with lightning. and i
swallow her whole as she pulls herself up from
youth, shaking off those early chicago years where
she and wright and others turned a chicago desert
into a well spring of words.

eyes. brilliant/solution eyes torpedoing the room
with sun. eyes/dressed like a woman. seeing thru
riddles. offering asylum from ghosts.

she stands over centuries as she talks. hands on
waist. a feminine memory washed up from another
shore. she opens her coat. a light colored blouse
dances against dark breasts. her words carved from
ancestral widows rain children and the room
contracts with color.

her voice turns the afternoon brown. this black
woman poet. removing false veils, baptizes us with
syllables. woman words. entering and leaving at
will:

> *Let a new earth rise. Let another world be born.*
> *Let a bloody peace be written in the sky. Let a*
> *second generation full of courage issue forth; let*
> *a people loving freedom come to growth. Let a*
> *beauty full of healing and a strength of final*
> *clenching be the pulsing in our spirits and our*
> *blood. Let the martial songs be written, let the*
> *dirges disappear. Let a race of men now rise and*
> *take control.**

walking back to my room, i listen to the afternoon.
play it again and again. scatter myself over evening
walls and passageways wet with her footprints.
in my room i collect papers. breasts. and listen
to our mothers hummmmming

* 'For My People' by Margaret Walker

to CHucK

i'm gonna write me
   a poem like
              e.e.
       cum
           mings to
               day. a
bout you
          mov
ing iNsIdE
          me touc
hing my vis
         cera un
      til i turn
in
  side out. i'
          m
go
  n n
      a   sc
      rew
   u on   pap   er
  cuz u
       3
       o
       o
       o
  mi

          awayfromme
my   MAN
        ca
        re
        ss   my   br
            ea
            sts   my
              bl
                    ack
ass
      rul
          ED   on   these
lin
      es.   they
                        yours.
yeah.
      imgonnawritemea
pOeM
          like
                e.
E.   cu
          MmIn
        gS   to
                    day   cuz
heknewallabout
                scr
                    EW
ing
on   WH
                        ite   pa   per.

a ballad for stirling street (to be sung)

For Amina and Amira Baraka

jest finished readen a book
    bout howard street
guess it had to be written
    bout howard street

now someone shud write one
    bout stirling street
show the beauty of blk / culture
    on stirling street
need to hear bout brothers
    TCB / en on stirling street
need to see sun / wrapped / sisters

    on that black street
need to see Imamu and Amina
    walken blue / indigo / tall
need to hear the loud harambees
    strike gainst the wall

jest finished readen a book bout
    howard street
i've read a whole lot of books like
    howard street
if each one of us moved to a
    howard street

and worked hard like they do on
    stirling street

wudn't be no mo howard sts at all
all the howard sts wud fall – fall – fall
and won't that be good.
                        yeh. yeh.
                        and won't that be good.
                            yeh.   yeh.   yeh.

personal letter no. 3

nothing will keep
us young you know
not young men or
women who spin
their youth on
cool playing sounds.
we are what we
are what we never
think we are.
no more wild geo
graphies of the
flesh. echoes. that
we move in tune
to slower smells.
it is a hard thing
to admit that
sometimes after midnight
i am tired
of it all.

a poem for my father

how sad it must be
to love so many women
to need so many black
perfumed bodies weeping
underneath you.
                        when i remember all those nights
i filled my mind with
long wars between short
sighted trojans & greeks
while you slapped some
wide hips about in
your pvt dungeon,
when i remember your
deformity   i want to
do something about your
makeshift manhood.
i guess
            that is why
on meeting your sixth
wife, i cross myself
with her confessionals.

insomnia

i hear the wind of graves moving the sky.
the hills level their priested black
toward the vehement morning.
pain swears above the city.
from galleries of night
unvarnished dreams ring past these giant cuts
and as i kiss the eunuch moon,
the earth is out of my eyes.

A Poem for Paul

your face like
summer lightning
gets caught in my voice
and i draw you up from
deep rivers
taste your face of a
thousand names
see you smile
a new season
hear your voice
a wild sea pausing in the wind.

Past

COME into Black geography
you, seated like Manzu's cardinal,
come up through tongues
multiplying memories
and to avoid descent
among wounds
cruising like ships,
climb into these sockets
golden with brine.

> because i was born
> musicians to two
> black braids, i
> cut a blue
> song for america.
> and you, cushioned
> by middleclass springs,
> saw ghettos
> that stretched
> voices into dust
> turned corners
> where people walked
> on their faces.
> i sang unbending
> songs and gathered gods
> convenient as christ.
> i am the frozen
> face, here my

face marches
toward new myths
while spring runs
green with ghosts.
i am the living
mask, here my
skin worn
with adolescence
peels like
picasso's planes
and the earth
in one fold of
permanence stares
at the skies

if i had a big piece of dust
to ride on, i would gather up my pulse
and follow disposable dreams
and all things being equal
they would pass into butterflies
& quiver in sprawling yellow.

Why

Why must i string my hate
like japanese lanterns
over our pulse?
A minstrel's pain sings
in my thighs
i walk long walks against you
while in my dreams
we are green clay
ripening on canvas.

Poem No. 1

my husband sits
buddha like
watching me weave my
self among the sad
young men of my time.
he thinks i am going
to run away.
maybe i will.

July

the old men and women
quilt their legs
in the shade
while tapestry pigeons
strut their necks.
as i walk, thinking
about you my love,
i wonder what it is
to be old
and swallow death each day
like warm beer.

Father and Daughter (I)

we talk of light things you and I in this
small house. no winds stir here among
flame orange drapes that drape our genesis
And snow melts into rivers. The young
grandchild reviews her impudence that
makes you laugh and clap for more allure.
Ah, how she twirls the emerald lariat.
When evening comes your eyes transfer
to space you have not known and taste the blood
breath of a final flower. Past equal birth,
the smell of salt begins another flood:
your land is in the ashes of the South.
perhaps the color of our losses:
perhaps the memory that dreams nurse:
old man, we do not speak of crosses.

poem at thirty

it is midnight
no magical bewitching
hour for me
i know only that
i am here waiting
remembering that
once as a child
i walked two
miles in my sleep.
did i know
then where i
was going?
traveling. i'm
always traveling.
i want to tell
you about me
about nights on a
brown couch when
i wrapped my
bones in lint and
refused to move.
no one touches
me anymore.
father do not
send me out
among strangers.
you you black man

stretching scraping
the mold from your body.
here is my hand.
i am not afraid
of the night.

Depression

I.

i have gone into my eyes
bumping against sockets that sing
smelling the evening from under the sun
where waterless bones move
toward their rivers in incense.
a piece of light crawls up and down
then turns a corner.

as when drunken air molts in beds,
tumbling over blankets that cover sweat
nudging into sheets continuing dreams;
so i have settled in wheelbarrows
grotesque with wounds,
small and insistent as sleigh bells.

am i a voice delighting in the sand?
look how the masks rock on the winds
moving in tune to leaves.
i shed my clothes.
am i a seed consumed by breasts
without the weasel's eye
or the spaniel teeth of a child?

2.

i have cried all night
tears pouring out of my forehead
sluggish in pulse,
tears from a spinal soul
that run in silence to my birth
ayyyy! am i born? i cannot peel the flesh.
i hear the moon daring
to dance these rooms.
O to become a star.
stars seek their own mercy
and sigh the quiet, like gods.

(section 1)

A poem for my brother (reflections on his death from AIDS: June 8, 1981)

1. death

The day you died
a fever starched my bones.
within the slurred
sheets, i hoarded my legs
while you rowed out among the boulevards
balancing your veins on sails.
easy the eye of hunger
as i peeled the sharp
sweat and swallowed wholesale molds.

2. recovery (a)

What comes after
is consciousness of the morning
of the licensed sun that subdues
immoderate elements.
there is a kindness in illness
the indulgence of discrepancies.

reduced to the ménage of houses
and green drapes that puff their seasons
toward the face.

i wonder what to do now.
i am afraid
i remember a childhood that cried
after extinguished lights
when only the coated banners answered.

3. recovery (b)

There is a savior in these buds
look how the phallic stems distend
in welcome.
O copper flowerheads
confine my womb that i may dwell within.
i see these gardens, whom i love
i feel the sky's sweat on my face
now that these robes no longer bark
i praise abandonment.

4. wake

i have not come for summary.
must i renounce all babylons?
here, without psalms,
these leaves grow white
and burn the bones with dance.
here, without surfs,
young panicles bloom on the clouds and fly
while myths tick grey as thunder.

5. burial

you in the crow's rain
rusting amid ribs
my mouth spills your birth
i have named you prince of boards
stretching with the tides.

you in the toad's tongue
peeling on nerves
look. look. the earth is running palms.

6. (on) (the) (road). again.

somewhere a flower walks in mass
purchasing wholesale christs
sealing white-willow sacraments.

naked on steeples
where trappist idioms sail
an atom peels the air.

O i will gather my pulse
muffled by sibilants
and follow disposable dreams.

Does Your House Have Lions?

sister's voice

this was a migration unlike
the 1900s of black men and women
coming north for jobs. freedom. life.
this was a migration to begin
to bend a father's heart again
to birth seduction from the past
to repay desertion at last.

imagine him short and black
thin mustache draping thin lips
imagine him country and exact
thin body, underfed hips
watching at this corral of battleships
and bastards. watching for forget
and remember. dancing his pirouette.

and he came my brother at seventeen
recruited by birthright and smell
grabbing the city by the root with clean
metallic teeth. commandant and infidel
pirating his family in their cell
and we waited for the anger to retreat
and we watched him embrace the city and the street.

first he auctioned off his legs. eyes.
heart. in rooms of specific pain.
he specialized in generalize
learned newyorkese and all profane.
enslaved his body to cocaine
denied his father's signature
damned his sister's overture.

and a new geography greeted him.
the atlantic drifted from offshore
to lick his wounds to give him slim
transfusion as he turned changed wore
a new waistcoat of solicitor
antidote to his southern skin
ammunition for a young paladin.

and the bars. the glitter. the light
discharging pain from his bygone anguish
of young black boy scared of the night.
sequestered on this new bank, he surveyed the fish
sweet cargoes crowded with scales feverish
with quick sales full sails of flesh
searing the coastline of his acquiesce.

and the days rummaging his eyes
and the nights flickering through a slit
of narrow bars. hips. thighs.
and his thoughts labeling him misfit
as he prowled, pranced in the starlit
city, coloring his days and nights
with gluttony and praise and unreconciled rites.

brother's voice

father. i despise you for abandoning me
to aunts and mothers and ministers of tissue
tongues, nibbling at my boyish knee.
father. forgive me for i know not what they do
moving me backwards through seams of bamboo
masks, staring eyes campaigning for
my attention. come O lords; my extended metaphor.

sister. i am not your true brother
one half of me resides in my mother's breast
in her eyes where tears exceed their worth.
the other half walks on tiptoe to divest
his tongue of me, this father always a guest
never a permanent resident of my veins
always a traveler to other terrains.

mother. i love you. you are my living saint
walking inside my skull you multiply out loud
in dainty dreams seraphim smiles without a tint
of mystery. you move among us with dark
gait intrepid steps that disavowed
retirement from an elaborate sex
while you prepared each morning's text.

the sermon for each day was my father
husband who left you shipwrecked with child
the movie of the week was my father
staring out from philco screens while your wild
dreams of nouveau lady genuflecting in single file
in a southern city of mouths on mascaraed thighs
twentieth century of elasticized lies.

what does a liver know of peace
or spleen. kidneys. ribs. be still my soul.
how does a city broker its disease
within the confines of a borough, where control
limps tepid – like carrying a parasol
of hurts, hurting, hurted, hurtful croons
stranded in measured arenas without pulpits or spittoons.

came the summer of nineteen sixty
harlem luxuriating in Malcolm's voice
became Big Red beautiful became a city
of magnificent Black Birds steel eyes moist
as he insinuated his words of sweet choice
while politicians complained about this racist
this alchemist. this strategist. this purist.

came the rallies sponsored by new york core
came Malcolm with speeches spilling exact and compact
became a traveling man who revived the poor
who answered with slow echoes became cataract
and fiesta became future and flashback
filling the selves with an old outrage
piercing the cold corners with a new carriage.

then i began an awakening a flowering outside
the living dead became a wanderer of air
barking at the stars became a bride
bridegroom of change timeless black with hair
moist with kinks and morning dare
then i began to think me alive with form and history
then i made my former life an accessory.

how to erect respect in a country of men
where dollars pump their veins?
how to return from exile from swollen
tongues crisscrossing my frail domain?
how to learn to love me amid all the pain?
how to look into his eyes and be reborn
without blood and phlegm and thorn?

father's voice

the day he traveled to my daughter's house
it was june. he cursed me with his morning nod
of anger as he filtered his callous
walk. skip. hop. feet slipshod
from 125th street bars, face curled with odd
reflections. the skin of a father is accented
in the sentence of the unaccented.

i was a southern Negro man playing music
married to a high yellow woman who loved my unheard
face, who slept with me in nordic
beauty. i prisoner since my birth to fear
i unfashioned buried in an open grave
of mornings unclapped with constant sight
of masters fattened decked with my diminished light.

this love. this first wife of mine, died in childbirth
this face of complex lace exiled her breath
into another design, and i died became wanderlust
demanded recompense from friends for my heartbreak
cursed the land for this new heartache
put her away with a youthful pause
never called her name again, wrapped my heart in gauze.

became romeo bound, applauded women
as i squeezed their syrup, drank their stenciled
face, danced between their legs, placed my swollen
shank to the world, became man distilled
early twentieth-century black man fossilled
fulfilled by women things, foreclosing on my life.
mother where do i go before i arrive?

she wasn't as beautiful as my first wife
this ruby-colored girl insinuating her limb
against my thigh positioning her wild-life
her non-virginal smell as virginal her climb
towards me with slow walking heels made me limp
made me stumble, made my legs squint
until i stopped, stepped inside her footprint.

i did not want to leave you son, this flame
this pecan-colored festival requested me
not my child, your sister. your mother could not frame
herself as her mother and i absentee
father, and i nightclub owner carefree
did not heed her blood, did not see my girl's eyes
shaved buckled down with southern thighs.

now my seventy-eight years urge me on your land
now my predator legs prey, broadcast
no new nightmares no longer birdman
of cornerstone comes, i come to collapse the past
while bonfires burn up your orphan's mask
i sing a dirge of lost black southern manhood
this harlem man begging pardon, secreting old.

i was told i don't remember who
i think i was told he entered his sister's house
cursed me anew, tried to tattoo
her tongue with worms, tried to arouse
her slumbering veins to espouse
his venom and she leaned slapped him still
stilled his mouth across early morning chill.

rumor has it that he slapped her hard
down purgatorial sounds of caress
rumor has it that he rushed her down a boulevard
of mad laughter while his hands grabbed harness –
like her arms and she, avenger and she heiress
to naked lightning, detonated him, began her dance
of looted hems gathering together for his inheritance.

blood the sound of blood paddling down the road
blood the taste of blood choking their eyes
and my son's body blood-stained red
with country-lies, city-lies, father-lies, mother-lies,
and my daughter clamoring to exorcise
old thieves trespassing in an old refrain
conjured up a blue-black chord to ordain.

wa ma ne ho mene so oo*
oseee yei, oseee yei, oseee yei
wa ma ne ho mene so oo
he has become holy as he walks toward daresay
can you hear his blood tissue ready to pray
he who wore death discourages any plague
he who was an orphan now recollects his legs.

* *wa ma ne ho mene so oo:* he is arising in all his majesty *oseee yei:* a shout of praise

family voices

————

ancestors' voices

brother's voice

there is nothing i do not comprehend
i have become a collector of shouts
hold my ears father, i have come to mend
our hearts raise a glass celebrate root out
lyrical slaughters become your only son devout
i have become a lover of sweet water
i worship stone i will not betray you father.

father's voice

steady your hand old man do not trouble
yourself with language, stalk his wound
he is listening to your corpuscles cradle
the clap and thunder of a new sound
he has called your name and old teeth are found
can you hold me son, as i rise from this whimper
can you hear me son, as i cross over this river.

father's voice

i am preparing for his coming, i sit on my flesh
i am wealthy my limbs free of moths
i am in praise of convalesce
i will stand free of the walking sabbaths
i will return sermons crowded with cloths
i am learning how to talk to my son's dust
i have tossed my net toward a future trust.

ancestor's voice (male)

do you remember me,	huh?
when our teeth were iron,	huh?
did you drum about me,	hey?
and not babylon,	hey?
did you take your weapon,	huh?
rattle it on any mattress,	hey?
til you became powerless?	hey, huh, heyyyyyyyy?

ancestor's voice (female)

do you remember me,   ayyyyyy?
when our wombs were cerebral,   ayyyyyy?
did you dream about me,   ayyyyyy?
and not betrayal,   ayyyyyy?
did you take your coastal
blood to any playground   ayyyyyy?
to every resident clown?   ayyyyyyyyyyyy?

sister's voice

let the spirit raise up echoes in my spine
brother. let our histories bleed no boomerangs
let my accent shrink the itch of undermine
brother. let our mouths speak without harangue
let my journey sing a path they sang
O i will purchase my brother's whisper.
O i will reward my brother's tongue.

ancestor's voice (female)

have you prepared a place of honor for me?
have you recalled us from death?
where is the *mmenson** to state our history?
where are the griots the food my failed breath?
where is the morning path i crossed in good faith?
what terror slows your journey to this dawn?
have you prepared a place for us to mourn?

* *mmenson:* orchestra of seven elephant tusk horns used on state occasions
to relate history

ancestor's voice (male)

water from my feet i return to you
oceans from my eyes to drown your bones
i am turning my heart away from you
hundreds of years have passed with no memorial stones
how can i forgive myself without the ritual horns?
your stool sits too long at this testimony
your stool forgets the flesh of ceremony.

brother's voice

i travel to India, father, Sai Baba says i must return
home seeking the light of the soft stone smile
i travel to India, father, Sai Baba says my turn
has come to prostrate pray reconcile
my soul with him who enters single file
i worship the light of the timid ground
i walk wide-eyed through blue slits of sound.

brother's voice

sister tell me about this marriage crown
you wear, tell me how to claim it all without fanfare
i want children, dreamers of the upside down
i want children screamers with kinky hair
i want a rocking chair child for my heir.
sister i want my tongue curling forward with this
while my face flows full with promise.

brother's voice

sister tell me about this cough i cough
all of my skin cradled in this cough
my body ancient as this white cough, i cough
all day and night i'm haunted by this cough,
a snake rattles in my throat this cough, i cough
a scream embalms my chest with cough
sister an echo surrounds my lungs with this cough, i cough.

brother's voice

i linger in stethoscopes and thermometers at Lenox Hill
i have entered the hospital to test
the cough and temperature making me ill
i have entered this hospital to rest
and all i have discovered is unrest
the doctor says happily it is not pneumonia or cancer
the doctor says my temperature is like a trickster.

ancestor's voice (male)

it is necessary to remember the sea
never forget how it leaps out of nowhere
it is necessary to remember the sea
holding your ancestors in a nightmare
of waves smooth breasts of warfare
is there no anguish no balm of Gilead for the dead?
is there no amulet for this coming dread?

ancestor's voice (female)

why won't you stand up
show us how to dare
why won't you stand up
investigate this nightmare
show us how to prepare
your children's eyes stand at attention
your children's eyes itch for resurrection.

ancestor's voice (female)

drink this tea
(bitter-heyyyyyy?) as bitter
as my bones hugging the sea
pour salt into the laughter
of eyes popping out of water
tears sail down my one eye
ornamental anger parts my smile.

sister's voice

come down to my house in philadelphia man
what you need is a cleansing of the body
come down to philadelphia where i can fan
your blood cool take custody
of your infection flood it into frailty
come down and i will defend your skin
against the threat of constant confession.

brother's voice

i checked myself out of the hospital
sister. i'm back at work on a new skyscraper
i'm piecing together the city in a recital
of steel and windows. no rice paper
walls here to destroy my design. no bootlegger
wires light this expensive east-side dwelling
up here, my limbs sequester themselves in lightning

father's voice

i'm leaving this message on your voice mail
your brother's back in the hospital temperature 105
i've called his mother, she arrives tomorrow wholesale
the doctors wait for me at every corner they arrive
with stationary voices tracking the sweat-hive
of his body embroidering needles on his veins
i pray his corpuscles learn how to abstain.

father's voice

where to go?
where to go today?
where to have gone at some ago
time when he was at play
in the world? what kind of day
is this where a son's body bleeds feces?
what kind of day anoints his flesh with effigies?

ancestor's voice (female)

i hear the water whistling in squads
of blue comings, the ocean has become a thief
i see our souls transported, lightning rods
of apocalyptic disbelief
the sea opens and shuts with our grief
new fathers have come to record their loss
old fathers know this accustomed chaos.

mother's voice

i am here my baby in your hospital room
i am here my love i have kissed your morning breath
i have walked around your father's gloom
i have come straight to see you grazing near death
you are hot at the edge of this city's wealth
the doctors praise your courage your ancestral smell
the doctors record your body's constant betrayal.

mother's voice

i have waited all day for this stepdaughter
i have made a special time for her voice
she is late, talking on her own to another doctor
i must prepare my tongue for the proper choice
of words, make my eyes full, moist.
i will let them operate on his diminished body
i will indulge their hands in this new fantasy.

daughter's voice

mothermothermother
dead when i was one
stepmotherstepmotherstepmother
alive with overdone
let his final days be a monotone
no cuttings no more stabbings of arms and legs
no resident tubes to collect these final dregs.

brother's voice

O forgive me mother
O forgive me father
O forgive me sister
O forgive me fever
O forgive me tremor
O forgive me rumor
O forgive me terror.

brother's voice

dress me in white
not hospital white
dress me in white
of my ancestor's white
of Sai Baba's white
of my morning white
of my spirit's white.

brother's voice

i am going out of my cell
i am ready
ring the bell (3 times)
i am ready
I have fitted my legs with mercy
my eyes say no requiem
mangi dem, *mangi dem, mangi dem*

---

* *mangi dem:* goodbye (i am going)

brother's voice

hold me with air
breathe me with air
sponge me with air
whisper me with air
comb me with air
brush me with air
rinse me with air.

brother's voice

i come. doctor.
mangi nyo*. captor.
i come. inventor.
mangi nyo. censor.
i come. preacher.
mangi nyo. confessor.
i come. ancestor.

* *mangi nyo:* i come

ancestor's voice

FEMALE	*jamma ga fanan**
MALE	look at his eyes. is he Asian?
FEMALE	*jamma ga fanan*
MALE	look at his hair. is he Indian?
FEMALE	*jamma ga fanan*
MALE	look at his cheekbones. is he Native American?
FEMALE	*jamma ga fanan*
MALE	look at his hands. is he African American?

* *jamma ga fanan:* good morning

ancestor's voice

FEMALE	*nyata**? how much is this death rattle?
MALE	*nyata?* he is not owned by anyone here or there.
FEMALE	*nyata?* how much for this bundle of applause circling his everywhere?
MALE	*nyata?* how much for the walking air?
FEMALE	*nyata?* how much for him to share this blue ash?
MALE	*nyata?* how much for him to share the calabash?

* *nyata:* how much

ancestor's voice

FEMALE   where are the gods when we need them?
MALE   they are stammering someplace off camera.
FEMALE   where are their masks, their substitute emblem?
MALE   they rustle in weeds like an old dilemma.
FEMALE   where is Buddha? Allah? Jehovah? Ptah? Ra?
MALE   will their tongues acknowledge us one day?
FEMALE   will their cobwebs remember us one day?

ancestor's voice (family)

TO BE SUNG

MALE	*sala maleikum*	hello
FEMALE	*nanga def*	how are you?
MALE	*sala maleikum*	hello
BROTHER	*magni fi rek*	i am well
BROTHER	*dama buga lek*	i want to eat
BROTHER	*dama buga naan*	i want to drink
MALE / FEMALE	*kaifi African*	come here African
MALE / FEMALE	*kai fi African*	come here African
BROTHER	*mangi nyo*	i am coming
BROTHER	*mangi nyo*	i am coming
BROTHER	*mangi nyo*	i am coming . . .

On Seeing a Pacifist Burn

this day is not
real. the crowing of
the far-away
carillons ring
out direction
less. even you are
un real roasting
under a man
hattan sky
while passersby flap
their indecent tongues.
even i am un
real but i
am black and
thought to be
without meaning.

malcolm

do not speak to me of martyrdom
of men who die to be remembered
on some parish day.
i don't believe in dying
though i too shall die
and violets like castanets
will echo me.

yet this man
this dreamer,
thick-lipped with words
will never speak again
and in each winter
when the cold air cracks
with frost, i'll breathe
his breath and mourn
my gun-filled nights.
he was the sun that tagged
the western sky and
melted tiger-scholars
while they searched for stripes.
he said, 'fuck you white
man. we have been
curled too long. nothing
is sacred now. not your
white faces nor any
land that separates

until some voices
squat with spasms.'

do not speak to me of living.
life is obscene with crowds
of white on black.
death is my pulse.
what might have been
is not for him / or me
but what could have been
floods the womb until i drown.

An Anthem

for the ANC and Brandywine Peace Community

Our vision is our voice
we cut through the country
where madmen goosestep in tune to Guernica.

we are people made of fire
we walk with ceremonial breaths
we have condemned talking mouths.

we run without legs
we see without eyes
loud laughter breaks over our heads.

give me courage so I can spread
it over my face and mouth.

we are secret rivers
with shaking hips and crests
come awake in our thunder
so that our eyes can see behind trees.

for the world is split wide open
and you hide your hands behind your backs
for the world is broken into little pieces
and you beg with tin cups for life.

are we not more than hunger and music?
are we not more than harlequins and horns?
are we not more than color and drums?
are we not more than anger and dance?

give me courage so I can spread it
over my face and mouth.

we are the shakers
walking from top to bottom in a day
we are like Shango
involving ourselves in acts
that bring life to the middle
of our stomachs

we are coming towards you madmen
shredding your death talk
standing in front with mornings around our waist
we have inherited our prayers from
the rain
our eyes from the children of Soweto.

red rain pours over the land
and our fire mixes with the water.

give me courage so I can spread
it over my face and mouth.

in the courtroom

and they were mostly
all blk/
          daid/dyin people
in the courtroom
                    they didn't
know it though.
                    i mean even those with
lawyers &
          sure/cases.
                              one defendant
confessed his guilt
                    of another crime
to avoid this one
                    here on stage rite
courtroom no. 6
                    and the wite judge
                    (fair one i'm told)
sed u've served 11 months & 1 day
that's enuff
          time fo that charge.
                                        and
the daid/dying/man
                    next to me
nods and
          nods
                    and nods   away
his life.   till those round him   cough

slight coughs.
              die small deaths
                                  inhale more smoke.
in the courtroom
              arena of our life.

MIAS

(missing in action and other atlantas)

this morning i heard the cuckoo bird calling
and i saw children wandering like quicksand
over the exquisite city
scooping up summer leaves in enema bags
self-sustaining warriors spitting
long metal seeds on porcelain bricks.

atlanta:
           city of cathedrals and colleges
           rustling spirituals in the morning air
           while black skulls splinter the nite
           and emmett till bones drop in choruses.

littleman. where you running to?
yes. you. youngblood.
touching and touched at random
running towards places where legions ride.

           yo man. you want some action.
           im yo/main man.
           buy me. i can give it to you
           wholesale.

heyladycarryyobagsfoyou?
50¢costyouonly50¢.yo.man.
washyocar.idoagoodjob.

heymanwhyyousocold?
yoman.youneedyobasement
cleaned?meandmypartner
doyoupdecent. yoman.

johannesburg:

      squatting like a manicured mannequin
      while gathering ghosts clockwise
      and policing men, using up their tongues
      Pronounce death syllables
      in the nite,

        august 18:
      30 yr. old african arrested
      on the highway. taken to
      port elizabeth. examined.
      found to be in good health.
      placed in a private cell
      for questioning.

        sept. 7:
      varicose cells. full of
      assassins, beating their
      red arms against the walls.
      and biko, trying to ration
      his blood spills permanent
      blood in a port elizabeth cell.
      and biko's body sings heavy
      with cracks.

        sept. 13:
      hear ye. hear ye. hear ye.
      i regret to announce that stephen

biko is dead. he has refused
food since sept. 5th. we did
all we could for the man.
he has hanged himself while sleeping
we did all we could for him.
he fell while answering our questions
we did all we could for the man.
he washed his face and hung him
self out to dry
we did all we could for him.
he drowned while drinking his supper
we did all we could for the man.
he fell

      hangedhimself   starved
drowned himself
we did all we could for him.
it's hard to keep someone alive
who won't even cooperate.
hear ye.

can i borrow yo/eyes south africa?
can i redistribute yo/legs america?
multiplying multinationally over the world.

      yebo madoda*
      yebo bafazi
      i say
      yebo madoda
      yebo bafazi

* *yebo madoda:* come on men and women

el salvador:

country of vowelled ghosts.
country of red bones
a pulse beat gone mad
with death.

redwhiteandblue guns splintering the nite with glass
redwhiteandblue death squads running on borrowed
knees cascading dreams.

quiero ser libre
pues libre naci
        i say
quiero ser libre
pues libre naci

they came to the village that nite. all day the
birds had pedaled clockwise drowning their
feet in clouds. the old men and women
talked of foreboding, that it was a bad sign.
and they crossed themselves in two as
their eyes concluded design.
they came that nite to the village.
calling peace. liberty. freedom.
their tongues lassoing us with
circus patriotism
their elbows wrapped in blood paper
they came penises drawn
their white togas covering their
stained glass legs
their thick hands tattooing decay
on los campaneros till their
young legs rolled out from under them

to greet death
they came leaving a tattoo of hunger
over the land.
          quiero ser libre
          pues libre naci
so i plant myself in the middle
of my biography
of dying drinking working dancing people
their tongues swollen with slavery
waiting and i say
yebo madoda
yebo bafazi
cmon men and women
peel your guerrilla veins toward
this chorus line of beasts who will sell
the morning air passing thru your bones
cmon. men. and. women.
plant yourself in the middle of your
blood with no transfusions for
reagan or botha or bush or
d'aubuisson.

plant yourself in the eyes of
the children who have died carving out their
own childhood.
plant yourself in the dreams of the people
scattered by morning bullets.
let there be everywhere our talk.
let there be everywhere our eyes.
let there be everywhere our thoughts.
let there be everywhere our love.
let there be everywhere our actions.
breathing hope and victory

into their unspoken questions
summoning the dead to life again
to the hereafter of freedom.

cmon. men. women,
i want to be free.

A Love Song for Spelman

For Dr Johnnetta B. Cole and Dr Camille Cosby

I.

What is a love song for Spelman?
Is it a pulse finding us each day at prayer?
If I am to take one voice which shall it be?
A voice stained like iron, dressed for feminine dreams?
What is a love voice for Spelman?
A song walking in tongues, rising and falling like butterflies?

2.

We begin.
With two women seeing the voice of God in the eyes of Black
    women.

We begin with newenglandschoolmarms
sisters of silver
creators of light.
Stoking the Southern fires with spit from their White skins.
We begin.

We begin.
With big lips
and dark skins
and woolly hair.

Itinerant eyes in expatriate hearts.
We begin.

We begin.
With a love for freedom
and a thirst for learning.
Tongues heavy with new words
from these our new world lepers.
We begin.

3.

In the long dark basement of shuttered sweat
we sat on benches harder than blue stone.
Some thought us an absurd gathering.
Eleven women of all ages
abundant with mornings.
Hands moving like wings toward knowledge
we came to the basement betrothed to dreams.
And we came to life again.

We came from being not human beings
but hands and feet opening and shutting
in institutionalized work.
We came being not women but trophies
and unremembered bodies hearing our voices in the
delirium of children.

And you told us, O Lord,
that we had to believe that you loved us.
And even though our bodies became stone
we loved you.

4.

We gathered up our skirts, our chins of lard,
from the dark basement to the barracks;
from two teachers to forty-two;
from eleven people to seven hundred;
from one classroom to a campus;
and our breaths agitated rooms and countryside,
became pure and sane and solid and we changed colors
like the seasons and
our hearts burned with fire and
not even the rust of Southern boundaries could stop us.

5.

Like ordained priests: ancient
walking in precise memory.
Like ordained warriors: majestic
Amazon women planting our songs
among the stars and on the waters.
Our songs from farms and cotton fields, from sugar
plantations and slums.
Our songs from urban and suburban roads.
Our songs from Alabama to Georgia, Brazil, and Harlem,
Washington, D.C., and the Congo.
Miracle songs.
Our songs clotting our blood when we bled.
Our songs sweet like eucalyptus against the silence.
Our songs freezing and burning, moving out of corners.
Remaking the air.

6.

Today.
We begin.
A second century of beginnings.
Daughters of great-granddaughters.
Daughters with eyes deeper than flesh.
We begin.
For we are always at the starting point.

We begin
today
with this woman, Johnnetta Cole. A Southern Black
woman.
And we hear her beginning voice
telling us that the dead are never dead.
Their breaths quiver in our shaking hips.
Their voices echo the dew laughing in trees.

We begin
with this woman.
Naming the world as she moves,
'Building for a hundred years hence, not only for today,'
leaving no piece of earth unbaptized.
And we children of all races, daughters from Mozambique
and Soweto, Florida and Mississippi, Cuba and Nicaragua,
outlive our mothers.
And hold our ancestral blood in our hands.

We begin
at this commencement
hearing our foremothers' voices calling to us.

'Listen, Sister Johnnetta. Sister Camille. Spelman sisters.
Listen: They made me give her up. My last child.
He came and took her and i screamed,
called out to Shango and Damballah and Olukun and Jesus
and Massa to jest let me hold on to her a whilst longer.
Just a few mo days til her eyes got usta seein
without me. But they took her anyways. They took her
whilst i wuz praying on my knees, and i walks slowly now,
my feet rooted to this earth, my footsteps echoin her
brown laughter . . .'

We begin today with these women. Camille Cosby and
Johnnetta B. Cole and all these past and present
Spelman women.
Smelling the evening from under the Sun.

We begin as they twist and turn,
as they call out to our Sister Aunties, Sister Mammies,
Sister Mamas, and tell them that their daughters and
sons dance in our veins. They have heard their
daughters' laughter in the wind.

These two women. These Spelman women. Shaping their
passion, involving themselves in work that brings life
to the middle of our stomachs – call out to our
ancestors to us and our children yet to be born.

*Ebe yiye.** *Ebe yiye. Ebe yiye.* For we have the tools now. We have
    the skills and the power. We have the love of self and of our
    people to make it better.

---

* *Ebe yiye: It'll get better.*

Ebe yiye. Ebe yiye. For you Mama dear. For you Mama Sukey moving in and out of plantation doors. For you Mammy Teena toiling in the noonday sun. For you young Mama strutting you big legs down 125th Street in Harlem. For you Lil Bits. Throat cut in a Chicago alley, for a fix.

Ebe yiye because of our love. Our unity, our strength. Our will. These two sister women. These Spelman sister women. Promise you it'll get better for you and me.

Ebe yiye. Ebe yiye. Ebe yiye. Ebeeee yiyeeee.

We begin.

Father and Daughter (II)

I.

it is difficult to believe that we
ever talked. how did we spend the night
while seasons passed in place of words? Outright
nothing is ever lost; save fantasy
that painted plastic walls with shades and
rolled soft violets while red fruit fell.
along your distant shore i heard you tell
of swollen dawns, and as you crossed the land
of stones you did not turn to sift the
mirror of my sands. This your caress.
in me the wings of owls who gathered flesh
began to turn and gave affinity
to skillful breaths that filled the air
with screaming. Who screams? life is everywhere.

2.

you cannot live here and bend my heart
amid the rhythm of your screams. Apart
still venom sleeps and drains down thru the years
touch not these hands once live with shears
i live a dream about you; each man
alone. You need the sterile woods old age can
bring, no opening of the veins whose smell
will bruise light breasts and burst our shell
of seeds. the landslide of your season
burns the air: this mating has no reason.
don't cry. late grief is not enough. the motion
of your tides still flows within: the ocean
of deep blood that drowns the land. we die:
while young moons rage and wander in the sky.

haikuography

From the moment i found a flowered book high up on a shelf at the 8th Street Bookshop in New York City, a book that *announced* Japanese haiku; from the moment i opened that book, and read the first haiku, i slid down onto the floor and cried and was changed. i had found *me*. It's something to find yourself in a poem – to discover the beauty that i knew resided somewhere in my twenty-one-year-old bloodstream; from the moment i asked the clerk in the bookstore if i was pronouncing this haiku word correctly, i knew that i had discovered me, had found an awakening, an awareness that i was connected not only to nature, but to the nature of myself and others; from the moment i saw the blood veins behind beautiful eyes, the fluids in teeth, and the enamel in tongues, i knew that haiku were no short-term memory, but a long memory.

Patricia Donegan shares the idea of 'haiku mind' – 'a simple yet profound way of seeing our everyday world and living our lives with the awareness of the moment expressed in haiku – and to therefore hopefully inspire others to live with more clarity, compassion, and peace.'

i knew when i heard young poets say in verse and conversation: i'm gonna put you on 'pause,' i heard their 'haiku nature,' their haikuography. They were saying, i gotta make you slow down and check out what's happening in your life. In the world.

So this haiku slows us down, makes us stay alive and breathe with that one breath that it takes to recite a haiku.

This haiku, this tough form disguised in beauty and insight, is like the blues, for they both offer no solutions, only a pronouncement, a formal declaration – an acceptance of pain, humor, beauty and non-beauty, death and rebirth, surprise and life. Always life. Both always help us to maintain memory and dignity.

What i found in the 8th Street Bookshop was extraordinary and *ordinary*: Silence. Crystals. Cornbread and greens. Laughter. Brocades. The sea. Beethoven. Coltrane. Spring and winter. Blue rivers. Dreadlocks. Blues. A waterfall. Empty mountains. Bamboo. Bodegas. Ancient generals. Lamps. Fireflies. Sarah Vaughan – her voice exploding in the universe, returning to earth in prayer. Plum blossoms. Silk and steel. *Cante jondo.* Wine. Hills. Flesh. Perfume. A breath inhaled and held. Silence.

And i found that my mouth and the river are one and the same.

i set sail
in tall grass
no air stirs.

Haiku

we grow up my love
because as yet there is no
other place to go

After the fifth day

with you
i pressed the
rose you brought me
into one of fanon's books.
it has no odor now.
                              but
i see you. handing me a red
rose and i remember
my birth.

Haiku

Was it yesterday
love we shifted the air and
made it blossom Black?

Haiku

O i am so sad, i
go from day to day like an
ordained stutterer.

10 haiku

for Max Roach

Nothing ends
every blade of grass
remembering your sound

your sounds exploding
in the universe return
to earth in prayer

as you drummed
your hands kept
reaching for God

the morning sky
so lovely imitates
your laughter

you came warrior
clear your music
kissing our spines

feet tapping
singing, impeach
our blood

you came drumming
sweet life on
sails of flesh

your fast beat
riding the air settles
in our bones

your drums
soloing our breaths into
the beat . . . unbeat

your hands
shimmering on the
legs of rain.

15 haiku

for Toni Morrison

We know so little
about migrations of souls crossing
oceans. seas of longing;

we have not always been
prepared for landings that held
us suspended above our bones;

in the beginning
there wuz we and they and others
too mournful to be named;

or brought before elders
even held in contempt. they were
so young in their slaughterings;

in the beginning
when memory was sound. there was
bonesmell. bloodtear. whisperscream;

and we arrived
carrying flesh and disguise
expecting nothing;

always searching
for gusts of life
and sermons;

in the absence
of authentic Gods
new memory;

in our escape from plunder
in our nesting on agitated land
new memory;

in our fatigue at living
we saw mountains cracking
skulls, purple stars, colourless nights;

trees praising our innocence
new territories dressing our
limbs in starched bones;

in our traveling to weselves
in the building, in the journeying
to discover our own deaths;

in the beginning
there was a conspiracy of blue eyes
to iron eyes;

new memory falling into death
O will we ever know
what is no more with us;

O will weselves ever
convalesce as we ascend into wave after
wave of bloodmilk?

9 haiku

for Freedom's Sisters

(Kathleen Cleaver)
quicksilver
panther woman speaking
in thunder

(Charlayne Hunter-Gault)
summer silk woman
brushing the cobwebs
off Southern legs

(Shirley Chisholm)
We saw your
woman sound   footprinting
congressional hallways

(Betty Shabazz)
your quiet face
arrived at a road
unafraid of ashes . . .

(Fannie Lou Hamer)
　　feet deep
　　in cotton you shifted
　　the country's eyes

　　　　(Barbara Jordan)
　　　　　Texas star
　　　　　carrying delicate words
　　　　　around your waist

(Rosa Parks)
　　baptizer of
　　morning light walking us away
　　from reserved spaces

　　　　(Myrlie Evers-Williams)
　　　　　　you rescued women and men
　　　　　　from southern subscriptions
　　　　　　of death

(Dr Dorothy Irene Height)

　　I

　　your words
　　helped us reconnoiter
　　the wonder of women

II
woman sequestered
in the hurricane
of herstory . . .

6 haiku

for Maya Angelou

You have
taught us how
to pray

your poems
yellow tattoos on the
morning dew

we dance
in the eye
of your pores

in a sudden
pause of breath
secrets unlock

you show us
how to arrange our
worldly selves

your poems
a landscape of
seabirds.

Haiku and Tanka for Harriet Tubman

1

Picture a woman
riding thunder on
the legs of slavery . . .

2

Picture her kissing
our spines saying *no* to
the eyes of slavery . . .

3

Picture her rotating
the earth into a shape
of lives becoming . . .

4

Picture her leaning
into the eyes of our
birth clouds . . .

5

Picture this woman
saying *no* to the constant
yes of slavery . . .

6

Picture a woman
jumping rivers her
legs inhaling moons . . .

7

Picture her ripe
with seasons of
legs . . . running . . .

8

Picture her tasting
the secret corners
of woods . . .

9

Picture her saying:
You have within you the strength,
the patience, and the passion
to reach for the stars,
to change the world . . .

10

Imagine her words:
Every great dream begins
with a dreamer . . .

11

Imagine her saying:
I freed a thousand slaves,
could have freed
a thousand more if they
only knew they were slaves . . .

12

Imagine her humming:
How many days we got
fore we taste freedom . . .

13

Imagine a woman
asking: *How many workers*
for this freedom quilt . . .

14

Picture her saying:
A live runaway could do
great harm by going back
but a dead runaway
could tell no secrets . . .

15

Picture the daylight
bringing her to woods
full of birth moons . . .

16

Picture John Brown
shaking her hands three times saying:
General Tubman. General Tubman. General Tubman.

17

Picture her words:
There's two things I got a
right to: death or liberty . . .

18

Picture her saying *no*
to a play called *Uncle Tom's Cabin*:
I am the real thing . . .

19

Picture a Black woman:
could not read or write
trailing freedom refrains . . .

20

Picture her face
turning southward walking
down a Southern road . . .

21

Picture this woman
freedom bound . . . tasting a
people's preserved breath . . .

22

Picture this woman
of royalty . . . wearing a crown
of morning air . . .

23

Picture her walking,
running, reviving
a country's breath . . .

24

Picture black voices
leaving behind
lost tongues . . .

25

Picture her
Painting rainbows on
A summerbent people

26

Picture a woman
Walking on freedom legs
A seaspray of life

personal letter no. 2

i speak skimpily to
you about apartments i
no longer dwell in
and children who
chant their dis
obedience in choruses.
if i were young
i wd stretch you
with my wild words
while our nights
run soft with hands.
but i am what i
am. woman. alone
amid all this noise.

Acknowledgements

The poems in this Selection have appeared in the following collections.

from *Homecoming* (1969)

To CHucK
poem at thirty
malcolm
personal letter no. 2

from *We a BaddDDD People* (1970)

a ballad for stirling street (to be sung)
personal letter no. 3
a poem for my father
in the courtroom

from *It's a New Day* (1971)

When we come
City Songs

from *Love Poems* (1973)

Sequences
Poem No. 10
Ballad
Poem no. 7
Why?
Poem no. 1
July
Father and Daughter
Haiku / After the fifth day
Haiku / Haiku

from *A Blues Book for Blue Black Magical Women* (1974)

Past

from *Homegirls and Handgrenades* (1984)

Story
A Poem for Paul
Depression
On Seeing a Pacifist Burn
Poem Written After Reading Wright's American Hunger
MIAS

from *Generations* (1985)

from a Black Feminist Conference
    Reflections on Margaret Walker : Poet
Father and Daughter

from *Under a Soprano Sky* (1987)

Under a Sporano Sky
At the Gallery of La Casa de Las Americas Habana. Dec. 1984
Fall
Philadelphia: Spring, 1985
insomnia
(section 1)

from *Wounded in the House of a Friend* (1997)

A Love Song for Spelman
This Is Not a Small Voice

from *Does Your House Have Lions?* (1998)

sister's voice
brother's voice
father's voice
family voices / ancestor voices

from *Like the Singing Coming off the Drums* (1999)

A Poem for Ella Fitzgerald

from *Shake Loose My Skin* (2000)

An Anthem
Fragment 1
Fragment 2

from *Morning Haiku* (2010)

haikuography
10 Haiku
15 Haiku
9 Haiku
6 Haiku
Haiku and Tanka for Harriet Tubman